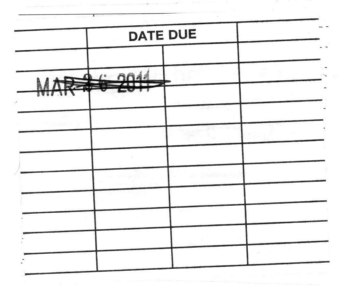

	DATE DUE		
	~~MAR 26 2011~~		

THE LIVING EARTH

WRITTEN AND ILLUSTRATED BY ELEONORE SCHMID

NORTH-SOUTH BOOKS / NEW YORK / LONDON

The earth is like a precious living thing, and it changes every day.
Some changes we can see. The ground turns to mud during
a spring rain and becomes very hard under the hot summer sun.

But many changes happen so slowly that we would never notice them. Each winter, water seeps into the sides of mountains and freezes, cracking the rock apart. Each spring, rains come and slowly wash the broken rock down the hill. After dozens, or hundreds, or thousands of years, the jagged rock that was once part of a mountain has become a smooth stone lying in the valley below.

The earth is made of many layers. The top layer, called topsoil, is the most fertile. Plants live in topsoil, as do millions of tiny animals. Beneath the topsoil are layers of clay, gravel, or sand. Under them are rocks and boulders. About fifty feet down is a layer of granite—the earth's crust.

When snow melts or rain falls, water soaks into the ground. As it filters through the topsoil, it is cleansed of impurities. The water collects in underground pools and rivers in the rocky crust. People drill wells to bring this clean, drinkable water to the surface.

Topsoil is made up, in part, of the decaying remains of dead plants and animals, called humus. When water soaks into soil, the minerals and nutrients stored in humus are released. Millions of seeds also lie buried in topsoil. The right combination of light, warmth, and moisture will cause the seeds to sprout. The sprouting seeds grow tiny roots, which draw in the minerals and nutrients.

As the plants grow, their leaves and stalks break the surface and reach for the warmth of the sun. At the same time, their roots grow in the opposite direction, deeper and deeper into the soil. The tangled roots of the plants help to protect the soil from the wind and the sun.

There are more living organisms in a single handful of soil than there are people on the entire earth. But you can't see most of what's living in the soil. The billions of bacteria, algae, fungi, and single-celled animals are too small to be seen without a microscope.

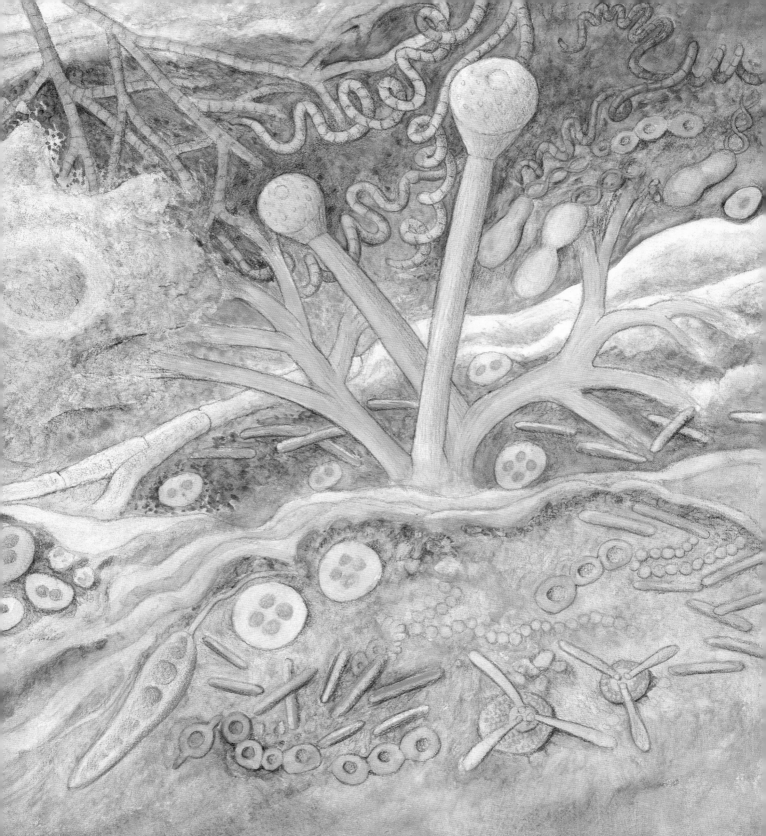

Eventually all living things, plant and animal, die and return to the earth. Over time, the microscopic organisms in the soil break down dead plants and animals into simple minerals and nutrients. When this process is complete, the humus is renewed, so that new seeds will sprout and new plants will grow. Nature is a cycle. Nothing is wasted, nothing is lost. The earth constantly renews itself.

Snails, beetles, ants, worms, and other insects and small animals live in or tunnel through the topsoil. When a plant or animal dies, these creatures feed on it. They begin the process of decomposition by breaking down dead matter.

Earthworms play a very important role in renewing the earth. These creatures burrow through soil, swallowing rotting plants and other matter. Whatever they cannot use is released. In this way earthworms help in decomposition. Their burrowing also loosens the soil, allowing air and water to reach the roots of plants.

Other animals live in the earth too. Mice and moles dig long tunnels. They gnaw at roots and eat insect larvae and worms. Rabbits live in burrows—complex networks of tunnels with many entrances and exits. Badger families live in similar underground homes.

Foxes and other larger animals raise their young in caves or hollows in the earth. They line their nests with straw and leaves, and store food for the long winter. Animals are warm and safe underground.

Much of the earth is covered with forests. Tree roots, like the roots of smaller plants, help hold soil together against floods and windstorms. Roots, dead leaves, moss, and grass in the forest all hold water. That is why it's usually cool and damp in a forest, even in summer.

Sometimes people cut down forests to make new fields for farms. Farmers till the fields and plant seeds, to grow grains, vegetables, and fruit. Some of the grain is fed to animals such as chickens, pigs, and cattle. And some farmland is used for dairy cows to graze on.

People need earth to produce food. So, year after year, farmers till the land. In spring the thawing earth is turned over, and the new crop is planted. In summer the crops are harvested. After the harvest, farmers sow plants to cover and protect the exposed earth.

When a plant is harvested, its nutrients do not return to the soil. To replace the lost nutrients, farmers spread manure and other fertilizers. They also plant a different crop in each field every year. By growing beans one year, alfalfa the next, and wheat after that, wise farmers do not wear out the earth.

To get a bigger harvest, some farmers put artificial fertilizers in the soil. They spray the crops with chemicals, to kill the insects and diseases that attack the plants. And some farmers grow the same crops year after year after year.

This way of farming may produce bigger harvests, but it also hurts the land. The tiny organisms that live in soil are harmed. Worms can't travel through the packed-down earth. The land is slowly drained of its nutrients, so more and more fertilizers are needed to produce new crops.

The earth holds many valuable resources, such as coal, iron, copper, and precious gems. But to find some resources entire mountains must be torn apart. To get at granite or other useful stone, huge quarries are dug into hillsides. Giant shovels are used to scoop gravel and sand out of the beds of lakes and rivers.

Entire forests are cut down to harvest the wood. Oil is pumped out of holes drilled deep in the ground. Natural gas flows through pipes that stretch across many miles of wilderness. What has taken nature millions of years to create is being used up by humans in a very short time.

In the city most of the earth is covered up by asphalt and
concrete. Buildings are often so close together that we can see the
earth only in parks and gardens. Here flowers and trees and grass
are allowed to grow.

The wind carries dust and tiny bits of soil through the air, dropping them everywhere. In a crack in the pavement, enough soil can come together for a plant to live in. First moss grows, then grass sprouts, and finally a flower blooms. Even the smallest patch of city soil can support the cycle of life.

After a hot sunny day the soil is warm and dry. After a rain
shower, it is cool and moist. Sit on the ground, and feel the earth
beneath you. Take a handful of soil. Let it slip through your fingers.
Notice how delicate and crumbly it is, and how good it smells.

If we don't misuse it, the earth will continue to give us everything we need to survive. The earth is our only home. The earth is constantly changing. The earth is like a precious living thing.